Read-About® Holidays

Holi

By Uma Krishnaswami

Consultant
Nanci R. Vargus, Ed.D.
Assistant Professor
Literacy Education
University of Indianapolis
Indianapolis, Indiana

CP Children's Press®
A Division of Scholastic Inc.
New York   Toronto   London   Auckland   Sydney
Mexico City   New Delhi   Hong Kong
Danbury, Connecticut

Designer: Herman Adler Design
Photo Researcher: Caroline Anderson
The photo on the cover shows a girl putting gulal on her mother during Holi.

Library of Congress Cataloging-in-Publication Data

Krishnaswami, Uma.
  Holi / by Uma Krishnaswami.
      p. cm. — (Rookie read-about holidays)
Summary: An introduction to the traditions and festivities of the Hindu
festival called Holi.
Includes index.
  .ISBN 0-516-22863-3 (lib. bdg.)   0-516-27764-2 (pbk.)
  1. Holi (Hindu festival)—Juvenile literature. [1. Holi (Hindu
festival) 2. Festivals.] I. Title. II. Series.
  BL1239.82.H65 K75 2003
  294.5'36—dc21
                                        2002015131

CHILDREN'S PRESS, AND ROOKIE READ-ABOUT®,
and associated logos are trademarks and or registered trademarks
of Grolier Publishing Co., Inc. SCHOLASTIC and associated logos
are trademarks and or registered trademarks of Scholastic Inc.

1 2 3 4 5 6 7 8 9 10 R 12 11 10 09 08 07 06 05 04 03

It is March in India. The
trees are blooming. Soon it
will be Holi (HOH-lee).

Holi is a Hindu (HIN-doo) holiday. The Hindu religion began in India.

Today, Hindu people live in many countries of the world.

5

March 2003

Sunday	Monday	Tuesday	Wednesday	Thursday	Friday	Saturday
						1
2	3	4	5	6	7	8
9	10	11	12	13	14	15
16	17	**18**	19	20	21	22
23	24	25	26	27	28	29
30	31					

Holi is celebrated on
a full moon in March.

The exact date changes
from year to year.

An old Hindu story tells
of a wicked princess
named Holika.

She had magic powers that
kept her safe from fire.

Once she tried to kill her good nephew.

She carried him into a big bonfire, but he did not get burned.

The gods took Holika's powers away, and she died.

A statue of Holika and her nephew

People in northern India light bonfires on the night before Holi.

Holi is celebrated to remind us that good wins over evil.

Holi also marks the coming of spring.

People clean and paint their houses to get ready for Holi.

They buy new, white clothes.

Holi day is here at last.

People put bright red dots
on each other's foreheads.
The dots are called *tika*
(TEE-kah).

People toss colored powder called *gulal* (goo-LAHL) on everyone they see.

On Holi day, you may throw gulal even on people you don't know.

People also toss colored
water at each other.

Some use a squirter called
a *pichkari* (pitch-KAH-ree).

Soon everyone is purple and orange and blue from head to toe. Bright white clothes have turned into rainbows.

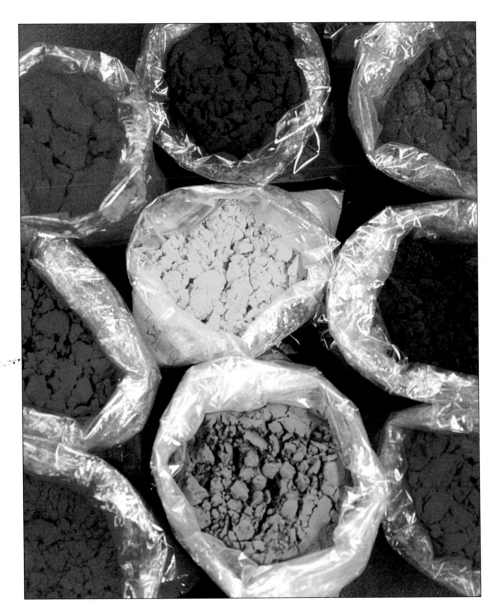

Gulal was once made from crushed flowers, seeds, and clay.

Now it contains dyes, and sometimes glitter.

Some people visit the
temple (TEM-pul) on Holi.

They promise to be good
friends and neighbors.

Families gather to eat special foods. They sing songs and tell stories.

They pass around sweets called *mithai* (mit-HA-ee).

"Sweeten your mouth," the grown-ups say.

27

28

Holi is one holiday when everyone can be a kid!

Words You Know

blooming

bonfire

friends

gulal

mithai

pichkari

tika

31

Index

clay, 23
crushed flowers, 23
dyes, 23
families, 26
foods, 26
friends, 25
full moon, 7
glitter, 23
gulal, 17, 23
Hindu religion, 4
Holika, 7, 8
March, 3, 7

mithai, 26
neighbors, 25
pichkari, 19
seeds, 23
songs, 26
spring, 11
temple, 24
tika, 14
trees, 3
water, 18
white clothes, 13, 20

About the Author

Uma Krishnaswami was born in New Delhi, India. She spent much of her childhood in the north and remembers celebrating Holi with neighbors and friends. She has written several books for young people. She lives with her husband and son in northwestern New Mexico.

Photo Credits

Photographs © 2003: Corbis Images: 16 (AFP), 12 (Jeremy Horner), 3, 30 top left (Earl & Nazima Kowall); Dinodia Picture Agency: 27, 31 top left (A.D. Cheoolkar), 25, 30 bottom left (HMA), 19, 31 bottom left (N.M. Jain), 10, 18, 30 top right (RSC), 28 (Manhusudan Tawde), 22, 30 bottom right (VHM); Photo Researchers, NY/Gilda Schiff-Zirinsky: 5; Stock Boston/ Peter Menzel: 21; The Image Works/DPA/SSK: cover; TRIP Photo Library/ H. Rogers: 13; Viesti Collection, Inc.: 9 (Dinodia Picture Agency), 24 (Joe Viesti); Visuals Unlimited/Inga Spence: 15, 31 right.